Lesson 1

1A Understanding Meanings p. 2

1. C
2. C
3. A **utopia** is a place or state of perfect conditions.
4. C
5. A **covert** act is one that is secret.
6. An **encomium** is an expression of praise.
7. An **acolyte** is a person who assists in religious services.
8. C
9. C
10. C
11. A **sedulous** effort is one that is completed with careful perseverance.
12. A **protagonist** is the chief character in a drama or story.
13. To **declaim** something is to recite it in the style of a public speech.
14. C
15. C

1B Using Words p. 3

1. b. declaim
2. b. obdurate
3. a. valedictory
   b. valedictory
4. b. bibulous
5. a. protagonist
6. a. coalesce
   b. coalesce
7. a. prescience
   b. prescience
8. c. sedulous

1C Synonyms, Antonyms, Analogies p. 5

1. valediction — salutation		A
2. secret — covert		S
3. flexible — obdurate		A
4. follower — acolyte		S
5. vague — trenchant		A
6. d	9. a	
7. b	10. c	
8. c		

vary.

iction.

*Applies to all Images of Words exercises.

1E Narrative p. 9 (*Sentences are examples; students' answers may vary.)

1. Ellison's characters are trying different ways to improve their circumstances. Their life is not perfect.
2. Because this character is one of the most important people in a work, one would expect that he or she would be named.
3. It is described as a **bibulous** get-together.
4. As Ellison thought about the sentence, ideas about his own identity **coalesced**.
5. As an **acolyte** he probably studied the ideas of the Brotherhood so that he could help Brother Jack in whatever work he had to do.
6. Ras is described as "the Exhorter"; this suggests he expressed his ideas in public speeches.
7. The events it describes are similar to events that would happen a decade or more later.
8. He gave the **valedictory** address and received a scholarship. The fact that he did well in his studies suggests he worked hard.
9. The narrative says he expressed his ideas in essays.
10. The narrative describes several different directions he tried. He refused to stay in a position if it did not work.
11. It did not receive the **encomiums** that *Invisible Man* received.

*Applies to all Narrative exercises.

Lesson 2

2A Understanding Meanings p. 12

1. C
2. A **congenital** issue is one that exists at or dates from birth.
3. **Élan** is a lively spirit with a distinctive style.
4. C
5. C
6. An **apothegm** is a short, instructive saying.
7. C
8. C
9. An **ineluctable** course is one that is inevitable.
10. C
11. C
12. To **absolve** someone is to clear someone of guilt.
13. C
14. Something that is **germane** is pertinent and fitting.
15. C

2B Using Words p. 13

1. a. immured
2. a. prototype
   b. prototype
   c. prototype
3. a. élan
   b. élan
4. a. adumbrate
5. b. invoked
6. No sentence suggests **congenital**.
7. a. germane
8. b. internecine
   c. internecine

2C Synonyms, Antonyms, Analogies p. 14

1. inherent — congenital		S
2. aspersion — defamation		S
3. dubious — ineluctable		A
4. irrelevant — germane		A
5. apothegm — maxim		S
6. b	9. c	
7. c	10. b	
8. c		

2D Images of Words p. 15

1. c	7. b
2. a, b	8. a, b
3. a, c	9. No sentence suggests **internecine**.
4. a, b, c	
5. c	
6. a	10. a, b, c

2E Narrative p. 18

1. Mental retardation may be **congenital** or may come about because of an accident or disease.
2. Answers will vary but probably will include **aspersions** made by unthinking or unkind people.
3. People are no longer **immured** in institutions.
4. Eunice Shriver wanted to give more opportunities to mentally retarded people; she knew from her sister's experience that nothing would change unless someone took action.
5. They have been the model for how the Special Olympics were organized.
6. He acted as **coadjutor** to Eunice Shriver
7. There are more possibilities today for people with mental retardation. They can participate in society in different ways. Before, they were viewed as being unable to do anything.
8. They are described as performing with an **élan** that was uncharacteristic of their behavior most of the time.
9. The help of thousands of volunteers and the pleasure of the athletes in participating in the events and in the ongoing special training programs have been pertinent to the success of the Special Olympics.
10. Answers will vary but may include that it would be a lot of work to prepare such an event more frequently. Having it less often might make it more difficult for the athletes to maintain their skills.
11. In both situations, the games provided a **hiatus** in people's lives that allowed relief from the pressures they ordinarily experienced.

Lesson 3

3A Understanding Meanings p. 22

1. C
2. C
3. **Antediluvian** customs are those that are old-fashioned.
4. C
5. C
6. A **savant** is a person with detailed knowledge in a specialized field.
7. C
8. An **ascetic** is a person who practices self-denial.
9. C.
10. To **obviate** something is to prevent it or make it unnecessary.
11. C
12. C
13. A **nostrum** is a medicine or remedy of dubious value.
14. C
15. C

3B Using Words p. 23

1. a. denizen
   b. denizens
2. a. amalgam
   b. amalgam
3. b. flora
   c. flora
4. a. perennial
   b. perennial
5. c. ascetic
6. a. obviate
   c. obviate
7. a. imbibe
   b. imbibe
8. b. doyenne
   c. doyen

3C Synonyms, Antonyms, Analogies p. 24

1.	savant — charlatan	A
2.	deadly — beneficent	A
3.	ongoing — perennial	S
4.	require — obviate	A
5.	contemporary — antediluvian	A

6. b
7. b
8. b
9. c
10. a

3D Images of Words p. 25

1. c
2. No sentence suggests **ascetic**.
3. b, c
4. a, b
5. a
6. b, c
7. a, b
8. a, b
9. a
10. a

3E Narrative p. 28

1. It is not likely that synthetic drugs will disappear even if more treatments are developed from plants. Plant sources are less reliable than those created completely in the laboratory.
2. The narrative says that the knowledge about plants was passed from one generation to the next. This means the plants were present over many years.
3. Researchers do not know how many plants exist there, so they can only estimate how many will be lost.
4. As many as sixty thousand plant species could be growing within the Amazon region.
5. He hoped to **imbibe** their knowledge.
6. The shamans' knowledge has been extremely useful to the health and well being of the people in their communities. It is not outdated.
7. Both had extensive knowledge of how to use plants for medicinal purposes.
8. Answers will vary but may include the following. He or she might receive advice from a **charlatan** who knew nothing about what he or she was doing. A person might receive **nostrums**, whose effectiveness was unproven.
9. **Doyen** seems appropriate because Schultes clearly spent a lot of time doing research in the field and made some important practical contributions to health care because of his knowledge.
10. Along with their **beneficent** properties, they possess harmful qualities if used incorrectly.
11. He lived among the people for extended periods of time.

Lesson 4

4A Understanding Meanings p. 32

1. An **indigent** person is one who is extremely poor or needy.
2. A **benighted** attitude is one that is morally or intellectually lacking.
3. A **bourgeois** is a member of the middle class.
4. C
5. A **laudable** objective is one that is praiseworthy.
6. **Approbation** is an expression of approval.
7. C
8. An **iconoclast** is one who attacks established beliefs, customs, or institutions.
9. C
10. C
11. C
12. To **eschew** something is to stay away from or shun it.
13. C
14. C
15. To **expatiate** is to speak or write about something in great detail.

4B Using Words p. 33

1. a. eschew
   b. eschew
   c. eschew
2. a. mandate
3. c. benighted
4. a. regurgitate
   b. regurgitated
5. a. empirical
   b. empirical
6. a. bourgeois
   b. bourgeois
7. b. ostensible
8. a. expatiated
   b. expatiated

4C Synonyms, Antonyms, Analogies p. 35

1.	approbation — criticism	A
2.	risible — solemn	A
3.	benighted — deficient	S
4.	belief — credo	S
5.	laudable — despicable	A

6. d
7. b
8. d
9. c
10. b

4D Images of Words p. 36

1. c
2. b, c
3. c
4. a
5. a, b, c
6. b
7. a, b, c
8. b
9. b
10. No sentence suggests **mandate**.

4E Narrative p. 39

1. She used **empirical** evidence from her work with children.
2. She believed they were able to learn some things whereas the view current at that time was that these children had no mental capacity. They were provided with food and shelter but nothing else.
3. Because boys and girls were preparing for different roles as adults, they were studying different subjects.
4. They might consider it **risible** or they might be **recalcitrant**.
5. He proudly attended the graduation ceremony at which she received a degree in medicine, the first awarded to a woman, in Italy.
6. He would have said that women and men have different roles to play and should be educated to fulfill those roles.
7. The school was set up for children of **indigent** families, not for those of the middle class.
8. She did not instruct her students with the expectation that they would then **regurgitate** what she had said. Instead, she believed children could learn many things on their own if provided the opportunity.
9. They gave her a **mandate** to set up other schools using the same approach.

Lesson 5

5A Understanding Meanings p. 43

1. C
2. A **microcosm** is a smaller version of a larger system.
3. C
4. A **stratagem** is a plan that uses trickery to achieve a desired outcome.
5. To **execrate** someone is to denounce that person.
6. C
7. A **vendetta** is prolonged adversity between two families.
8. C
9. C
10. To **dissemble** is to hide information from someone in order to deceive that person.
11. C
12. An **egregious** act is one that is exceptionally offensive.
13. To **carouse** is to take part in boisterous merrymaking.
14. C
15. A **paroxysm** is a sudden outburst or unexpected occurrence.

5B Using Words p. 44

1. b. egregious
   c. egregious
2. c. pecuniary
3. c. contentious
4. a. archaic
   b. archaic
5. b. stultify
   c. stultify
6. b. microcosm
7. b. stratagem
8. a. paroxysm
   b. paroxysm

5C Synonyms, Antonyms, Analogies p. 45

1. fealty — loyalty	S
2. blatant — egregious	S
3. revel — carouse	S
4. chicanery — rectitude	A
5. maneuver — stratagem	S

6. b	9. c
7. b	10. b
8. b	

5D Images of Words p. 46

1. c	6. No sentence suggests **paroxysm**.
2. a, b	7. c
3. b	8. a, b
4. a, b	9. a
5. a, c	10. b, c

5E Narrative p. 50

1. Each contrada has an ancient foe, which it **execrates** and toward whom it will take any action to insure its defeat.
2. The winning contrada does not receive money but rather the pleasure of triumphing over its traditional enemy.
3. During the year they act with **rectitude**, but during the Palio they use whatever **chicanery** they can to defeat their rival contrade.
4. There once were practical reasons for the **stratagems** that are practiced before the race, but today these actions are carried on for the sake of tradition.
5. The bribery and **dissembling** that go on before the race reflect the essential skills the Sienese of the medieval period needed just to survive as a city when threatened by their powerful neighbors.
6. The narrative says that the Palio allows the people to express strong emotions and violent feelings; this seems to have reduced the crime rate.
7. The rival might feel a **paroxysm** of jealousy, anger, or frustration.
8. Answers will vary.
9. The contrada that is the traditional enemy of the winning contrada would probably find it difficult to celebrate.

Lesson 6

6A Understanding Meanings p. 53

1. C
2. A **presentiment** is a premonition of an event.
3. C
4. **Genealogy** is the study of family histories.
5. A **brackish** substance is one that is salty or unpleasant to the taste.
6. A **dissertation** is a long paper written for a college degree.
7. C
8. A **dolorous** occasion is one that is sad.
9. C
10. A **ramification** is the result of an idea or plan.
11. C
12. C
13. C
14. C
15. C

6B Using Words p. 54

1. b. presentiment
2. a. fecund
   b. fecund
   c. fecund
3. a. cognitive
   b. cognitive
4. b. insidious
   c. insidious
5. a. brackish
   b. brackish
6. a. torpid
7. a. inebriated
8. b. endemic

6C Synonyms, Antonyms, Analogies p. 56

1. consequence — ramifications	S
2. lucid — inebriated	A
3. fecund — barren	A
4. forerunner — precursor	S
5. dolorous — jovial	A

6. b	9. d
7. d	10. a
8. d	

6D Images of Words p. 57

1. No sentence suggests **brackish**.	5. c
	6. a, c
	7. b
2. a, c	8. a
3. b	9. a, c
4. a, b	10. a, c

6E Narrative p. 60

1. These are the first **insidious** signs of the disease, even though for many people such occurrences are normal and develop into nothing.
2. She and her father carried out intense lobbying and fund-raising for research. Wexler participated in gathering the information needed to make the discovery of the gene itself.
3. It could be the **precursor** to a cure.
4. She completed her doctoral **dissertation** on this topic.
5. It is described as **brackish**, which means somewhat salty.
6. A person only acquires the disease through inheriting a gene from a parent.
7. The narrative says that, at first, the residents viewed Wexler as an **interloper**, someone who was interfering in other people's affairs.
8. Symptoms that accompany the disease such as loss of **cognitive** skills and appearing **inebriated**, when not, are frightening. People need help to go forward.
9. In this isolated community where one woman had the gene, a small number of people intermarried. The people were **fecund** so there were more opportunities for the gene to appear.
10. People whose parents have the disease must make the difficult decision about whether they themselves want to be tested for the gene.

Lesson 7

7A Understanding Meanings p. 63

1. C
2. To **vitiate** something is to stultify it.
3. C
4. C
5. An **amorphous** object is shapeless.
6. C
7. C
8. A **variegated** surface is one that has mixed textures or colors.
9. C
10. C
11. C
12. A **mélange** is an amalgamation.
13. To **ratify** something is to give it approval.
14. To **abjure** a decision is to relinquish it.
15. C

7B Using Words p. 64

1. a. amorphous
   b. amorphous
   c. amorphous
2. a. exemplar
   b. exemplar
   c. exemplar
3. b. vitiate
4. a. nefarious
   c. nefarious
5. a. abjure
   b. abjure
6. b. mélange
   c. mélange
7. a. subsumed
   b. subsumed
8. a. inchoate
   c. inchoate

7C Synonyms, Antonyms, Analogies p. 65

1. hostility — animus S
2. diverse — variegated S
3. standard — exemplar S
4. exclude — subsume A
5. nihilistic — optimistic A
6. b
7. c
8. d
9. a
10. c

7D Images of Words p. 66

1. b
2. a, b, c
3. a, c
4. a, c
5. b
6. a, c
7. a
8. a, b
9. a
10. c

7E Narrative p. 69

1. They use a **mélange** of languages.
2. Their work is described as focusing on the economic, cultural, and social issues of Chicanos.
3. A mosaic emphasizes the **variegated** nature of the individual parts encompassing the whole. In a mosaic the parts retain their individuality.
4. Although they are citizens of this country and participate in its customs, their heritage, culture, and language come from another country. At times, these two influences may pull Chicanos in different directions.
5. Rivera's ideas of conservation, struggle, and invention in relation to culture imply a value to life and a belief that humans can have an effect on their surroundings.
6. Many have joined street gangs.
7. Rivera came from a poor family but through education and effort achieved a position where he could help others. His model for action was expressed by the words *conservation, struggle*, and *invention*.
8. When people are prevented from using their language, the culture that it expresses and embodies is **vitiated**.
9. Through this treaty the United States took over land that had been part of Mexico. This action could easily cause Mexicans to feel resentment.
10. He hoped he could channel the **inchoate** rage of young people he knew into more productive forms of action, such as writing.
11. When the Treaty of Guadalupe Hidalgo was ratified in 1848, that section of land was transferred from Mexico to the United States.

Lesson 8

8A Understanding Meanings p.72

1. C
2. A **cetacean** is whole or related marine mammal.
3. C
4. An **appurtenance** is an accessory.
5. C
6. C
7. C
8. To **purvey** something is to supply it.
9. To **decry** something is to express disapproval of it.
10. **Misapprehension** is misconception.
11. A **leviathan** is herculean in size.
12. To **abrogate** a treaty is to revoke it.
13. C
14. C
15. A **waiver** is documentation showing that a claim has been forgone.

8B Using Words p. 73

1. a. leviathan
   c. leviathan
2. b. purvey
   c. purvey
3. b. bivouac
   c. bivouac
4. a. cetacean
   b. cetacean
5. a. abrogate
6. a. recourse
   b. recourse
7. b. misapprehend
   c. misapprehend
8. b. mawkish

8C Synonyms, Antonyms, Analogies p. 75

1. aboriginal – native S
2. open-minded — parochial A
3. usefulness — desuetude A
4. appurtenance — implement S
5. claim — waive A
6. d
7. b
8. b
9. c
10. b

8D Images of Words p. 76

1. a
2. a, c
3. a, c
4. a, b, c
5. No sentence suggests **abrogate**.
6. a
7. b
8. b, c
9. a, b, c
10. b

8E Narrative p. 79

1. Whales are a source of food and vitamin C as well as materials for tools, clothing, and shelter.
2. They use rifles to complete the kill.
3. These people are described as **mawkish** for being overly sentimental about whales.
4. The Inuit are an **aboriginal** people. The ban did not apply to them because they used their catch to sustain life.
5. The waters near their settlement were **replete** with fish that attracted larger marine mammals. The Inuit had a rich supply of food.
6. A number of Inuit continue to hunt in the early spring for whales, bears, and walrus. The Inuit continue to make use of the animals they hunt as a source of food and other necessities.
7. Some groups want it to **abrogate** its ban and to allow more whaling. Other groups want a moratorium on all whaling.
8. Answers will vary.
9. Although they live in a remote area of the world, their livelihood is affected by decisions made by groups of people far away from them.
10. Answers will vary but may include the idea of trying to raise popular support for their situation and of appealing to the International Whaling Commission.

Lesson 9

9A Understanding Meanings p. 85

1. To **exculpate** someone is to free that person from blame.
2. C
3. C
4. A **lateral** movement is one that is made sideways.
5. C
6. C
7. A **heterogeneous** group is one whose members are diverse.
8. **Calumny** is intentional slander.
9. C
10. To **enervate** someone is to weaken that person.
11. A **viviparous** creature is one that produces live young.
12. An **epicure** is one who loves fine food.
13. C
14. C
15. C

9B Using Words p. 86

1. a. exculpated
2. b. quintessential
   c. quintessential
3. a. domain
   b. domain
   c. domain
4. a. veritable
5. c. infinitesimal
6. b. apposite
7. a. epicure
   c. epicure
8. a. primeval
   c. primeval

9C Synonyms, Antonyms, Analogies p. 87

1. enervate — enliven A
2. infinitesimal — enormous A
3. domain — territory S
4. smooth — serrated A
5. exculpatory — incriminating A
6. b
7. d
8. c
9. c
10. a

9D Images of Words p. 88

1. c
2. a, c
3. c
4. a, c
5. a, b
6. a, b
7. a
8. No sentence suggests **quintessence**.
9. a, b
10. No sentences suggest **exculpate**.

9E Narrative p. 91

1. No, it is not. Out of 350 species, only about a dozen are known to attack humans.
2. The white shark possesses **lateral** sensors which allow it to detect movements by swimmers or fish; it also has the ability to detect the presence of another creature through the electrical field given off by that being.
3. The narrative says that sharks were present in the **primeval** seas millions of years ago.
4. The meat has too high a concentration of uric acid to be edible.
5. The narrative says there are sharks six inches long as well as fifty feet long. Some sharks eat plankton and others eat meat.
6. They are both **serrated**.
7. This shark can detect **infinitesimally** small quantities of blood because of its acute sense of smell.
8. They might see the **dorsal** fin protruding from the water.
9. Sharks are **viviparous**, bearing live young instead of producing eggs.
10. Human ignorance is one. The narrative says humans know very little about sharks. In addition, movies perpetuate this ignorance by portraying sharks as evil creatures that purposely attack humans.
11. Millions of sharks die each year when they are caught unintentionally in long-line fishing nets. They have also been killed in large numbers for their fins, which are used in shark-fin soup.

Lesson 10

10A Understanding Meanings p. 94

1. C
2. A **wraith** is a ghostly apparition.
3. C
4. C
5. C
6. A **sycophant** is a flatterer.
7. C
8. C
9. A **nonplussed** person does not know what to do next.
10. To be **askew** is to be crooked or misaligned.
11. C
12. A **prodigal** is a wasteful person.
13. C
14. C
15. A **peripatetic** beggar is one who walks from place to place.

10B Using Words p. 95

1. a. askew
   b. askew
   c. askew
2. b. apotheosis
   c. apotheosis
3. a. nonplussed
4. b. acumen
5. a. erstwhile
   c. erstwhile
6. a. vacuous
   c. vacuous
7. b. chasten
   c. chasten
8. a. prodigal

10C Synonyms, Antonyms, Analogies p. 96

1. alert — vacuous A
2. peripatetic — stationary A
3. frugal — prodigal A
4. acumen — cleverness S
5. askew — crooked S
6. b
7. d
8. b
9. c
10. b

10D Images of Words p. 97

1. b
2. a, b
3. b
4. a, b
5. b, c
6. a
7. a, b
8. b
9. b
10. b

10E Narrative p. 100

1. His business **acumen** combined with his ability as a commercial artist allowed him to earn a lot of money.
2. He had a **wraith**like appearance and a **vacuous** gaze. But he was stronger and more alert than he appeared.
3. The narrative says his wig was often **askew**.
4. He wanted to be famous.
5. He stopped seeing many of his **erstwhile** companions, and he increased security at the Factory.
6. Answers will vary but may include that he was famous and many people are attracted to being around celebrities. If flattery allows them to do this, they may act in this way.
7. His death was quite unexpected. People probably did not know what to say.
8. The opening of the museum devoted to his work was a kind of **apotheosis**.
9. After his death, the things that he had bought were sold. People paid much higher prices for them than they were worth simply because Warhol had owned them.
10. His presence and influence are still felt today. He has had more than fifteen minutes of fame.
11. He blurred the **demarcation** between commercial art and fine art by treating commercial art as fine art and then reproducing it in quantity.

Lesson 11

11A Understanding Meanings p. 103

1. C
2. C
3. A **supplicant** is one who pleads for something.
4. C
5. C
6. **Obloquy** is the denunciation of shameful actions.
7. C
8. To **temporize** is to avoid purposely an action or a decision in order to gain time.
9. C
10. A **filial** relationship is one between a parent and a child.
11. To **fulminate** is to attack verbally.
12. A **nugatory** matter is one of no consequence.
13. C
14. C
15. C

11B Using Words p. 104

1. a. polemic
   c. polemic
2. a. nugatory
   b. nugatory
3. a. confreres
   c. confreres
4. a. palpable
   b. palpable
   c. palpable
5. b. supplicate
6. a. obloquy
7. a. convoke
8. a. peruse
   c. peruse

11C Synonyms, Antonyms, Analogies p. 106

1. melodious — cacophonous A
2. delay — temporize S
3. dismiss — convoke A
4. jocular — solemn A
5. supplicate — plead S
6. b
7. c
8. a
9. c
10. b

11D Images of Words p. 107

1. b
2. c
3. a
4. a, b
5. b
6. c
7. b
8. No sentence suggests **polemic**.
9. a
10. b, c

11E Narrative p. 110

1. The senator from Oregon **fulminated** that giving women the vote "would make every home a hell on earth."
2. The amendment guaranteeing women the right to vote was passed by the Senate.
3. It states that they were getting **fractious** in the 100-degree heat.
4. She didn't hesitate to put pressure on her son with her direct message: ". . . . vote for suffrage."
5. He feared their **obloquy** should he vote according to his belief.
6. Women would have been denied legal **parity** with men on voting rights.
7. The narrative says that he **perused** her letter.
8. She appealed to his **filial** devotion.
9. Harry Burn's vote rendered their efforts **nugatory**.
10. It states that the tension in the chamber was **palpable**.
11. "A **cacophony** of mingled cries of shock and joy, cheers and jeers, applause and hisses erupted."
12. They invited no women to the **convocation** that certified the Nineteenth Amendment.
13. It expresses a forced attempt at **jocularity**.

Lesson 12

12A Understanding Meanings p. 113

1. C
2. A **salutary** treatment is one that is healthful.
3. C
4. C
5. A **depraved** person is one who is morally corrupt.
6. To be **morbid** is to be affected by gloomy thoughts.
7. C
8. C
9. **Omniscience** is the complete awareness of what is going on.
10. A **colloquy** is a formal conversation or dialogue.
11. C
12. C
13. To **apprise** someone is to alert them to, or inform them of, something.
14. C
15. C

12B Using Words p. 114

1. No sentence suggests **colloquy**.
2. a. morbid
   c. morbid
3. a. deprave
4. a. apprised
   c. apprised
5. a. palliative
   c. palliative
6. a. beatific
7. a. preternatural
   b. preternatural
   c. preternatural
8. a. cogent
   b. cogent

12C Synonyms, Antonyms, Analogies p.116

1. preternatural — extraordinary S
2. apprise — elucidate S
3. hellish — infernal S
4. aggravating — palliative A
5. discrete — separate S
6. c
7. d
8. d
9. d
10. a

12D Images of Words p.117

1. a, c
2. a
3. a, c
4. No sentence suggests **inferno**.
5. b
6. No sentence suggests **cogent**.
7. b
8. No sentence suggests **colloquy**.
9. b, c
10. b, c

12E Narrative p.120

1. In this narrative, the Nazis are the best example of this word.
2. Elizabeth Kubler-Ross could never **efface** these sights from her memory.
3. No. Her attitude was one of **beatific** peacefulness.
4. Often doctors in the United States acted **omniscient** about patients' wishes when they decided whether to **apprise** them of their condition.
5. She held **colloquies** with them in which she listened as well as spoke.
6. Kubler-Ross identified five stages, each of which is distinct from the others.
7. Her work is a **cogent** expression of her ideas.
8. It had a **salutary** effect on the way the terminally ill are treated.
9. They cannot be cured, but they can be made more comfortable.
10. When asked about her impending death, she replied that she regarded it as a beautiful thing.

Lesson 13

13A Understanding Meanings p. 124

1. C
2. A **foible** is a small fault or weakness.
3. C
4. C
5. To **exhume** something is to dig it out of the ground or to recover it.
6. To **extirpate** something is to destroy it completely.
7. C
8. C
9. C
10. A **dilettante** is a person with a superficial knowledge of a field of study.
11. To **descry** something is to discern it.
12. C
13. C
14. To **adjure** someone is to advise the person to do something.
15. A **portal** is a door or entrance, which is usually large.

13B Using Words p. 125

1. b. portal
2. a. exhume
   c. exhume
3. a. abut
   b. abuts
4. a. restitution
5. c. extirpate
6. b. propitiated
7. b. descry
8. b. adjured
9. c. adjured

13C Synonyms, Antonyms, Analogies p. 126

1. bury — exhume A
2. ancestor — progenitor S
3. irritate — propitiate A
4. command – adjure S
5. violation — desecration S
6. d
7. b
8. a
9. b
10. a

13D Images of Words p. 127

1. c
2. c
3. a, b, c
4. b
5. a, b
6. No sentence suggests **restitution**.
7. b
8. a, c
9. a
10. b

13E Narrative p.130

1. It could be considered an act of **restitution** for previous attempts to **extirpate** Native-American culture.
2. Her Lenape **progenitors** were near that spot when they **descried** the ships of the first European settlers.
3. Congress chose a site that **abuts** the National Air and Space Museum.
4. Its **portals** lend a grand and dignified air to the entrance as visitors approach it.
5. His collecting was merely a rich man's **foible**, and he remained a **dilettante** when it came to understanding Native-American culture.
6. The Heye Foundation became **insolvent**.
7. The **desecration** offended Qualla Boundary Cherokee, Lynne Harlan, who offered daily prayers to **propitiate** the wounded spirits of the dead.
8. At school she was **adjured** to speak English and beaten if she spoke in her native tongue.
9. The speaker's remark suggests a tone of **jocularity**.

Lesson 14

14A Understanding Meanings p. 133

1. C
2. An **acerbic** article is one that uses a sarcastic or biting tone.
3. A **paean** is a hymn of praise or joy.
4. C
5. **Dotage** is a mental deterioration associated with old age.
6. C
7. To **deign** is to condescend to do something.
8. C
9. **Sartorial** concerns are those having to do with clothing.
10. C
11. C
12. C
13. A **canard** is a false story that is meant to mislead.
14. C
15. A **debonair** person is one who has an elegance of manner and appearance.

14B Using Words p. 134

1. b. svelte
2. a deign
3. a. repartee
4. a. dotage
5. a. paean
6. b. foist
7. b. overweening
   c. overweening
8. a. misconstrued
   b. misconstrue

14C Synonyms, Antonyms, Analogies p. 135

1. repine — celebrate A
2. deign — condescend S
3. slovenly — debonair A
4. narcissistic — modest A
5. insipid — pungent A
6. b
7. c
8. b
9. a
10. c

14D Images of Words p.136

1. b, c
2. a
3. a, c
4. b, c
5. b
6. No sentence suggests **svelte**.
7. b, c
8. a, c
9. a
10. b

14E Narrative p. 139

1. She **misconstrued** the other actors' embarrassment at her **insipid** performance as awe.
2. She could not have succeeded without talent and **overweening** ambition.
3. Rather than **deign** to appear in roles she found unacceptable, she bought out her contract from RKO.
4. It was cruel and funny at the same time.
5. The narrative says RKO **foisted** roles upon her.
6. Both became **sartorial** trademarks of their respective wearers.
7. The two stars would likely receive **paeans** from the public.
8. She retained her **svelte** figure all her life.
9. It began with **repartee**.
10. She might have gone into seclusion and retired from acting altogether.
11. The report would be a **canard**.

Lesson 15

15A Understanding Meanings p. 142

1. C
2. An **apiary** is a place where bees are raised for honey.
3. C
4. A **prospectus** is a printed statement giving information on a business for sale.
5. A **vernal** pool is one that appears in the spring of the year.
6. **Minutiae** are small details.
7. C
8. A **motley** collection is one composed of diverse and various elements.
9. C
10. **Exigencies** are demands or requirements.
11. An **archetype** is the original model of a particular type.
12. A **gustatory** treat is one that appeals to the sense of taste.
13. C
14. **Fatalism** is a view that one cannot affect events in any way.
15. C

15B Using Words p. 143

1. a. archetype
   b. archetype
2. a. exigencies
   c. exigencies
3. b. anachronism
   c. anachronism
4. No sentence suggests **fatalistic.**
5. c. checkered
6. a. motley
   b. motley
7. b. prospectus
8. a. devolve

15C Synonyms, Antonyms, Analogies p. 144

1. original — archetype S
2. motley — homogeneous A
3. demands — exigencies S
4. uneventful — checkered A
5. details — minutiae S
6. a
7. c
8. a
9. c
10. b

15D Images of Words p.145

1. a, c
2. b
3. b
4. b, c
5. a, c
6. b
7. a
8. a, b
9. No sentence suggests **carcinogen**.
10. b

15E Narrative p. 148

1. It should describe the regulations of the enterprise as well as reasonable expectations for the participants.
2. It offers **gustatory** delights that supermarket produce cannot equal.
3. The small farm is an American **archetype**.
4. It comes at the end of winter and signals the beginning of the growing season.
5. Their food is free of pesticides that may be **carcinogenic**.
6. The family farm would have become an **anachronism**.
7. The **exigencies** of managing a CSA operation require it.
8. They would want an **equitable** distribution system.
9. **Minutiae** such as filing papers or sorting mail are two possibilities.
10. The narrative states the movement has had a **checkered** past.
11. CSA members are described as a **motley** group.
12. They might start an **apiary** on the farm they belong to.

Lesson 16

16A Understanding Meanings p. 152

1. C
2. **Verisimilitude** depicts realism.
3. C
4. C
5. A **thespian** is a person who acts.
6. C
7. A **fetid** room is one with an offensive odor.
8. C
9. A **minion** is a follower.
10. C
11. An **apocalyptic** story is one that foretells terrible events.
12. A **decree** is a command.
13. C
14. C
15. A **staccato** delivery is one that has clear breaks and brief, distinct sounds.

16B Using Words p. 153

1. a. convulsions
   c. convulsions
2. a. staccato
   b. staccato
   c. staccato
3. a. decree
   b. decree
4. b. sanguinary
5. c. verisimilitude
6. a. apocalyptic
   c. apocalyptic
7. a. fetid
8. c. minions

16C Synonyms, Antonyms, Analogies p. 154

1. benevolent — sanguinary A
2. minion — follower S
3. sybaritic — ascetic A
4. verisimilitude — falsity A
5. spasm — convulsion S
6. c
7. d
8. a
9. d
10. c

NOTE TO TEACHERS: Please alert students to an error in the directions for the Hidden Message on page 161 of the Student's Book. The last sentence should read: If the exercise is done properly, the shaded boxes will spell out a quotation by the American playwright Jean Kerr.

16D Images of Words p. 155

1. a, c
2. No sentence suggests **apocalyptic**.
3. a
4. No sentence suggests **convulse**.
5. c
6. a, b
7. b, c
8. b, c
9. b
10. b

16E Narrative p. 158

1. Most of them enjoyed **sybaritic** lifestyles.
2. No. The narrative says that he was not **insouciant**.
3. The **minion** of Pol Pot, who burst into Dr. Ngor's operating theatre, began the **concatenation** of events that cost Dr. Ngor his relative freedom.
4. Both were **sanguinary** despots who created holocausts killing millions of people.
5. He ruled by **decree**.
6. Both were **apocalyptic** events in world history.
7. He identified it by its **staccato** sound.
8. Persons were killed for the **slightest** infraction of his rules.
9. These conditions would make the prison **fetid**.
10. He was part of a community of Cambodian **expatriates**.
11. He was given a part in a film by a Los Angeles movie-casting director.
12. They praised it for its **verisimilitude**.

Lesson 17

17A Understanding Meanings p. 165

1. C
2. A **cynosure** is something that is the center of attention.
3. A **paragon** is a model of perfection.
4. C
5. C
6. **Symbiosis** is two organisms living together in a way that is beneficial for both.
7. C
8. A **tyro** is a beginner in any field.
9. To **abnegate** something is to denounce it.
10. A **perquisite** is a benefit one receives in addition to regular pay.
11. C.
12. To act with **celerity** is to act quickly.
13. C
14. C
15. **Badinage** is light, joking conversation.

17B Using Words p. 166

1. b. bedizened
   c. bedizened
2. a. milieu
   c. milieu
3. a. symbiotic
   b. symbiotic
4. c. perquisite
5. a. lissome
   b. lissome
6. a. abnegated
   c. abnegated
7. a. celerity
   c. celerity
8. b. cynosure
   c. cynosure

17C Synonyms, Antonyms, Analogies p. 167

1. bedizen — embellish	S
2. setting — milieu	S
3. abnegate — assume	A
4. celerity — swiftness	S
5. staid — flamboyant	A

6. d	9. a
7. b	10. d
8. a	

17D Images of Words p. 168

1. a, b	6. a, c
2. a, b, c	7. c
3. a	8. a
4. a, c	9. b, c
5. No sentence suggests **obstreperous**.	10. a, c

17E Narrative p. 171

1. Answers will vary but may include that she is not a model of perfection but is a good model showing how to come back after making mistakes.
2. Because of the alliance between these forces, more things are required of a tennis player than playing excellent tennis. He or she needs to be chosen by a management company and then to fulfill the requirements of the contract. It also helps if the person is appealing to television audiences.
3. They would want players who are **lissome** and who are highly motivated
4. It is one of high pressure where a few people are **cynosures**.
5. Tennis was a **staid** sport, but television viewers look for excitement.
6. They **bedizen** their clothing with company logos so that television viewers will associate the product with the athlete.
7. The narrative says she became **obstreperous** and quarreled publicly with her father.
8. Instead of receiving a modest sum for the use of their name, tennis professionals began to receive huge amounts of money for advertising products.
9. Answers will vary but may include that their **celerity** in signing her as a thirteen-year-old and dropping her when she got into trouble as a seventeen-year-old may have been wise in business terms but not very responsible in human terms.
10. Answers will vary but may include that the pressures such young people would face should be postponed. Their education could suffer because of the crowded **itinerary** and the **ancillary** activities related to tennis.

Lesson 18

18A Understanding Meanings p. 175

1. C
2. C
3. A **ghoulish** subject is one that is gruesome.
4. C
5. A **coma** is a state of deep unconsciousness.
6. C
7. A **consanguineous** relationship is one that is based on having a common ancestor.
8. An **onus** is a difficult responsibility or obligation.
9. A **nuptial** planner is one who advises on weddings.
10. C
11. A **cadaver** is a corpse.
12. C
13. A **nadir** is a low point.
14. C
15. To **arrogate** something is to take claim to it without having the right to do so.

18B Using Words p. 176

1. b. sanguine
   c. sanguine
2. a. infringes
   c. infringes
3. a. ghoul
   c. ghoulish
4. a. abortive
5. a. protocol
   b. protocol
6. c. cadaverous
7. c. onus
8. a. cerebral
   b. cerebral

18C Synonyms, Antonyms, Analogies p. 177

1. arrogate — relinquish	A
2. successful — abortive	A
3. corpse — cadaver	S
4. conscious — comatose	A
5. infringe — trespass	S

6. c	9. c
7. b	10. c
8. b	

18D Images of Words p. 178

1. b
2. a
3. c
4. b, c
5. b, c
6. a, b
7. a
8. b
9. b, c
10. No sentence suggests **cerebral**.

18E Narrative p. 181

1. **Lassitude** was one of the symptoms of the disease.
2. They were **consanguineous** with Anissa.
3. Their hopes were at their **nadir** when the two-year search for a donor ended without success.
4. The narrative says the **nuptials** took place when Marissa was two years old.
5. The body often rejected the organ until drugs became available that overcame the body's response.
6. Answers will vary but may include that such organs are viable only if they are removed from a **cadaver** that is only recently dead.
7. These patients cannot be removed from life-support systems if there is **cerebral** activity.
8. The state **arrogates** to itself the right to harvest organs from a body to save another life.
9. Answers will vary.

Lesson 19

19A Understanding Meanings p. 184

1. C
2. An **effulgent** stream is one that is radiant and glistening.
3. C
4. C
5. **Taciturnity** is a tendency to say little.
6. An **exegesis** is a critical interpretation of something.
7. C
8. **Mores** are accepted customs of a group or society.
9. C
10. A **miscreant** is a villain.
11. C
12. An **appellation** is a descriptive name given to a person or thing.
13. A **nemesis** is a powerful opponent who usually wins.
14. C
15. A **mordant** essay is one expressed in a sharp and penetrating style.

19B Using Words p. 185

1. a. efflorescence
   b. efflorescence
2. b. prolix
3. b. limn
   c. limn
4. a. exegesis
   c. exegesis
5. a. mores
   b. mores
6. c. miscreant
7. a. nemesis
   c. nemesis
8. a. genre
   c. genre

19C Synonyms, Antonyms, Analogies p.186

1. dim — effulgent A
2. decline — efflorescence A
3. caustic — mordant S
4. paragon — miscreant A
5. taciturn — prolix A
6. c
7. a
8. b
9. c
10. d

19D Images of Words p. 187

1. a, c
2. a
3. No sentence suggests **peccadillo**.
4. c
5. c
6. a, c
7. b
8. a, b
9. c
10. c

19E Narrative p. 191

1. The narrative says that the decade of the 1920s was the comic strip's golden age.
2. It was the first newspaper supplement to use color.
3. Characters were **prolix** in the beginning and became more **taciturn** over time.
4. His actions are described as **peccadilloes** or minor offenses. He wasn't a villain.
5. Answers will vary. The narrative says their **conjugal** life was marked by many small arguments but that these were not serious.
6. It has been made into movies, a radio show, and a Broadway musical.
7. At the time that she was created, most comic-strip characters were boys. For that very reason, the cartoonist decided to create a female lead. If the cartoonist had stayed with a boy, the character may have been called "Little Orphan Andy."
8. Their faces were drawn to match their peculiar names.
9. Comic strips like "Peanuts" and "Pogo" had a **didactic** element that was new.
10. It is an example of the **mordant** humor of Walt Kelly's "Pogo."

Lesson 20

20A Understanding Meanings p. 194

1. C
2. An **insular** person is one who is resistant to new ideas.
3. To **educe** something is to work it out through reasoning.
4. C
5. A **talisman** is an object believed to have magical powers.
6. C
7. **Mayhem** is the infliction of deliberate destruction on someone or something.
8. C.
9. C
10. A **terrestrial** means of transportation moves on earth.
11. C
12. To **preclude** an event is to prevent it.
13. A **rapacious** person is one who is greedy.
14. C
15. C

20B Using Words p. 195

1. a. parlous
   c. parlous
2. a. happenstance
   c. happenstance
3. a. educe
   c. educe
4. a. terrestrial
   b. terrestrial
   c. terrestrial
5. a. rapacious
   b. rapacious
6. b. mayhem
   c. mayhem
7. a. sublimate
8. a. preclude
   c. preclude

20C Synonyms, Antonyms, Analogies p. 196

1. changeable — equable A
2. restoration — despoliation A
3. positive — beneficent S
4. allow — preclude A
5. propinquity — proximity S
6. b
7. b
8. c
9. a
10. c

20D Images of Words p. 197

1. b
2. b
3. b, c
4. b, c
5. a, b, c
6. b, c
7. c
8. a, c
9. c
10. a, b

20E Narrative p. 200

1. The three volcanoes were in close **propinquity**.
2. The absence of maps or navigational devices in 400 AD **precluded** its being discovered by design.
3. The narrative says that the waters around the island were **pellucid** and that the climate was **equable**.
4. Palm trees were abundant on the island.
5. For fifty generations it was cut off from contact with the outside world.
6. The different groups **sublimated** their aggression in building more and larger statues.
7. They show that the Rapa Nui people were in a **parlous** state.
8. The fate of the island with its population and environmental pressures hints at the possible fate of the earth.
9. Answers will vary but may include the destruction of the rain forests, the disappearance of many species of plants and animals, and the contamination of the rivers, oceans, and air.

Lesson 4

Crossword Puzzle

1 E	X	P	A	2 T	I	3 A	T	E		4 E	S	5 C	H	6 E	W					7 D
N				R		S						R		A		8 C	A	I	R	O
9 C	O	A	L	E	S	C	E		10 C	O	V	E	R	T		H				Y
O				N		E						D				I		11 L	I	E
M		12 R		C		T				13 A		O				N		A		N
14 I	R	I	S	H		15 I	M	B	I	B	E			16 H	17 I	A	T	U	S	
U		S		18 A	B	C				S					L			D		19 P
M		I		N			20 I	21 N	V	O	K	E		22 F	L	23 O	R	A		U
	24 A	B	E	T				O		L			25 S			B		B		T
26 S		L						27 S	A	V	A	N	T			V		L		A
28 P	R	E	S	C	I	29 E	N	T		E			30 I	N	D	I	G	E	N	T
E						L		R					L			A				I
E						31 A	D	U	M	B	R	A	T	E		T				V
32 D	E	N	I	Z	E	N		M					S		33 B	E	F	O	R	E

page 41

Lesson 8

Hidden Message

ABORIGINE
TORPOR

EGREGIOUS
VITIATE
WAIVE
DECRY
DISSEMBLE

PRECURSOR
SUBSUME

RECTITUDE
INCHOATE
ENDEMIC

DICHOTOMY
CETACEAN
S
STRATAGEM

CHICANERY
VENDETTA
INVIDIOUS

MAWKISH
VARIEGATED

STULTIFY
DESUETUDE
BIVOUAC
DOLOROUS
PECUNIARY

LEVIATHAN
NIHILISM
PURVEY

REPLETE
MELANGE
ANIMUS
CAROUSE
RECOURSE
COGNITIVE

BRACKISH
RATIFY
FEALTY
EXEMPLAR
EXECRATE
W
ABJURE
INTERLOPER
INSIDIOUS

pages 81–83

Lesson 12

Crossword Puzzle

1 P	O	2 L	E	M	I	3 C		4 P	5 A	L	P	6 A	B	L	E		7 A			8 D
E		A				A			P			S					L			O
R		9 C	O	G	E	N	T		P			K		10 J	11 O	C	U	L	A	R
U		H				O		12 F	O	R	T	E			S		M			S
13 S	E	R	R	A	T	E	14 D		S			W			L		N			A
E		Y					I		I		15 L		16 P	R	O	17 D	I	G	A	L
		M		18 I			S		T		A					I				
19 P		20 O	M	N	I	S	C	I	E	N	T		21 E	22 P	I	C	U	R	23 E	
I		S		F			R				E			L		T			F	
24 C	R	E	T	E		25 T	E	M	26 P	O	R	I	Z	E		U			F	
N				R			T		U		A			N		27 M	E	D	A	L
I				N			28 E	X	C	U	L	P	A	T	E				C	
29 C	O	N	V	O	K	E			K					Y					E	

page 122

Lesson 16

Hidden Message

CARCINOGEN

DOTAGE
H
PROPITIATE
EXIGENCIES
CHECKERED

INSIPID
MINUTIAE
INSOUCIANCE
CANARD
THESPIAN
NARCISSISM
DESCRY

ARCHETYPE
REPARTEE
JOCOSE

REPINE
HOLOCAUST

ANACHRONISM
CORNUCOPIA
DEVOLVE
OVERWEENING
S

ABUT
ADJURE
DILETTANTE

MOTLEY
FOIBLE
EXHUME

DESECRATE
INFRACTION
MISCONSTRUE

CONVULSE
DEIGN
PAEAN
PORTAL
VERNAL

APIARY

APOCALYPTIC
DEBONAIR
EQUITABLE

FETID
EXPATRIATE
SARTORIAL
MINION

FOIST
STACCATO
EXTIRPATE
SVELTE
U
ACERBIC
DECREE

pages 161–163

Lesson 20

Crossword Puzzle

1 A	2 B	N	E	G	A	3 T	E		4 L	I	5 S	S	O	M	6 E			7 V		8 L
	E					A			A		Y				D		9 L	I	M	A
	D					C			S		10 M	A	Y	H	E	M		E		S
11 D	I	D	A	C	T	I	C		S		B				N		12 O	N	U	S
	Z					T		13 M	I	L	I	E	U					N		I
	E					U			E		O			14 M	O	15 R	D	A	N	T
16 I	N	S	U	L	A	R					T					A				U
N						17 N	E	18 M	E	S	I	S				D		19 P		D
F			20 P		21 O			O			C		22 B	A	D	I	N	A	G	E
23 R	E	F	R	A	C	T	O	R	Y			24 N				A		R		
I			O		T			E				25 A	N	26 C	I	L	L	A	R	27 Y
N			L		A			28 S	29 T	A	I	D		O				G		A
G		30 L	I	M	N				I			I		M				O		L
E			X		31 E	D	U	C	E		32 A	R	E	A		33 G	E	N	R	E

page 202